To my friend, Dean

[illegible]

19 August 1999

Hog killers and Other poems

by

Vernon Schmid

Poetry:
ISBN 0-89002-349-2 **$13.95**

Acknowledgements

Many of the poems in this collection were published in their original form elsewhere We are grateful to the following for their permission to reprint: ***The Maryland Poetry Review***, ***Fodderwing, Main Street***, ***Cecil County Magazine*** *(e-zine)*, ***The Bassettown Review. The Wooster Review, Bouillabaisse, The Poet's Attic, Brown Bag Review, The International Christian Digest, Living Poets Society*** (e-zine), ***Sisters Today, Alive Now!*** and ***The Eleventh Muse.***

Library of Congress Catalogue Card Nmber: 99-62270

Northwoods Press
Thomaston, Maine
U.S.A.

For Susan

Geography blended with time equals destiny.

\- Joseph Brodsky

Hog Killers

[After reading Gunter Grass' "Novemberland."]

[On November 9, 1923, the Bavarian Beer Hall Nazi plot was foiled and Hitler was imprisoned. On November 9, 1938, Jewish shops and homes were vandalized by Nazi mobs, the date becoming known as Kristallnacht, the night of the broken glass. On November 9, 1989 - The Berlin Wall fell.]

1

November is hog killing month.
On our farm in southeast Kansas,
my father would bring water to boil
in a fifty-five gallon barrel placed
over an open fire. In the hog pen
we cornered a frightened hog fattened
especially for this autumn occasion.
Stunned by a sledge hammer blow
the bewildered creature would stagger
and fall as my father moved quickly to cut
its throat in one easy motion. Blood
spurting from the severed artery, the hog
kicked and quivered its way to death.
In November I hear the hogs squeal.
The spurt of fresh red blood spills
across the soil of my distant memory.

2

In the November of my ninth year,
young boys, sons of hog killers,
pinned me down in the school yard.
With dirty playground fingers, they peeled
back my eye-lids, their venomous voices
urging the sun to come burn my retinas
into darkness, calling me Nazi and traitor.
Their voices called for judgment to strike me,

to end my confused and fragile life.
I did not know the depth of their hate.
On tear-filled journeys home through marshy
pastures I wondered how, at the age of nine,
I might secretly be a part of something evil,
something I did not know or understand.
It was a puzzle for my time. It introduced
me to mystery, called me to grace.

3

A dog-day Kansas child, I never thought myself
German although it was grandfather's tongue.
Now I read about the Novembers and the nines of history and
realize blood ties the November nine counters to me
hard and fast as stone. My names stand
solid as the trees my ancestor's adored.
They are strong names breathing deep
within my Germanic heart and soul.
At four, trying to read, already a dreamer,
my skinny overall clad body kicking up
dust beneath callused feet, a stick horse
snorting its impatience through my nostrils
as I rode it hard to the ground, I did not
hear the crack and crunch of distant glass.
Kristallnacht only came to my heart and mind
forty years later, like an unexpected relative
dropping by after a long unexcused absence.
Today with the crunch of dying leaves
underfoot, the smell of wood smoke in the air,
memories of fresh sausage tipping their hat
to my taste buds, I remember it all.
I wonder at uncles and cousins who
carried their skin cased blood and bones
back to the Rhineland, to the ancestral home
Some to die, others to come home scarred.
And on November 9, my aging heart and head
Seeks to know to whom payment is due.

Hunted Man

"Repentance is for little children."
- Thomas Merton

In the nineteenth year of acne and night sweats
I left the persistent sand blowing across the flats
below Cheyenne Mountain, its shining weapons
glistening with anguish, the laughter of night
women in Colorado Springs bars ringing
harshly in my once virgin and no longer ears.
What I remember most is the pocked face,
pale and hollow eyed, staring into the barrel
of my cocked and ready sawed-off shotgun.
The prisoner and me, the military policeman,
staring at one another with eyes of death.
His singular voice, spewing venom and hate,
speaks to me even now as it spoke to me then.
"Someday," it says, echoing across the decades,
"I will find you and, by God, I will kill you!"
For forty years I waited and watched for him.
Then, at a Days Inn by Arlington National Cemetery,
he finally found me. His face was changed.
He was grey and overweight and I noted
he tired easily. But, he got my attention.
He took his fist and hit me hard in the chest
as I stood beside the motel ice machine. No coward,
I took the blow like a man and then fell,
my heart thundering. I realized he had found me
three times before. I had not known him then.
But, that day he smiled the cold grin of scores settled.
I looked into those hollow eyes and saw him nod,
a smug recognition of our final race together.
No longer do I have to look over my shoulder
in shopping malls or busy Philadelphia streets.
That day, gazing at him with my hard policeman eyes,
I saw him laugh and I knew the secret of his vow.

Arrowhead

Pointed to drive the shaft
deep in the dark flesh,
blood and sinew bursting
to death, this flint
endures long after man
drove it between
bison ribs, tasting
the throbbing heart ripped
fresh from the fallen,
praising the Creator
of stone and bison.

Osage Questa

[With the exception of a tiny strip called the Cbautauqua Hills and the small southeast corner region called the Cherokee Lowlands, the Osage Questas of Kansas are bordered roughly on the north by the Wakarusa River, the south by Oklahoma, the east by Missouri, and the west by U.S. 99, and are marked by the Neosho River running through the beart of the region. - Kansas Geological Survey]

1.

Limestone pushes its jagged head
up beneath this physiographic province,

where eastern slopes are steeper
than their sleeping western sisters.

Refugees from the henge.
Kansas plowbreakers, hiders of bones,

markers of graves, these rocks sky
point like granite arrows counting off in winter

when stones crack like a Sharps carbine
bringing the last buffalo shaggily down.

Beyond the ken of prairie visionaries,
children stand, oak still, listening,

as rattle-trap ragged death whispers
names, deep as parched throats

beneath dark and bloody ground
where small, freckled boys once struck

steel to stone, measuring hardness
against the vacant gaze of old men.

2.

Like these stones, the People
remain part of this hard, dark land.

Their images are as real as the river
pushing its way toward the Mississippi.

The People knew the stones, shaped
them for points to bring the deer down.

Now, soil, newly turned by spring plowing,
offers up their arrowheads and pottery shards,

where once, the People huddled by smoking
cottonwood fires cooking venison,

when luck slept with the tired hunters.
Darkened by feces and urine, the fields

are now turned by shining plows
to expose treasures for the bending.

And now and then a whoop shatters
the silence of the field over a found point,

a fractured remnant, while silent ghosts
watch from behind gooseberry bushes,

where the creek turns its private way.

Nude Swimmers

When I dream of her white skin
naked against the moon's nether side,
droplets falling from her lips as she
rises up out of the still dark water,
her face remains young as memory
caught in time by a Kansas pond.

I suppose she no longer swims at night.
She is, no doubt, a settled Wichita wife
with daughters away at university
where young men dream of them
swimming nude in the Kansas midnight.

Pie-Plate People

Aristophanes claimed early human beings
were round, pie-plate round, possessing
four hands, two feet, one head, two faces
peering opposite ways, four ears listening.

Four hands fondled two private members.
Of the pie-plate people there were three kinds.
One was male to male. One was male to female.
One was female to female. All possessed power.

Such power struck fear into the hearts of gods.
Zeus, the story goes, called together a godly jury.
They found a solution. Divide and conquer.
Every pie-plate person was divided into two.

Split like apples for the eating, or half-moons,
soft, white underbellies exposed to the enemy,
pie-plate people disturbed the fragile peace.
They began to seek out one another.

And discovering their other halves they threw
their arms wide to take one another into wholeness.
Sometimes one could not find the other.
So, they starved, one sided and shriveled as flounder.

Vernon Schmid

Coplas On the Journey Toward

[A Memorial Poem for My Parents, 1985]

From the beginning,
the elders say,
something in me
did not seek to fit.

Always round
in a square peg hole,
refusing to mesh
with predestination's cogs,
heart roaring
behind quiet smiles
waiting for a time,
to reveal the vision
that from the first,
the elders say,
did not seek to fit.

Now, I kneel.
Break the loaf.
"Body of Christ."
Lift the cup.
"Blood of Christ."
Heart and bread
broken as Christ.

Five of 45 nuclear protesters charged witb trespassing during a demonstration at General Electric's Valley Forge Space Center have been convicted and fined.

Caught among holy fools,
pacifist crazies,
demented priests,
and poets
where peace
is the ritual
maintained
as sacramental fire
in cathedrals
where altars

splashed with blood
foreshadow the lamb
waiting for last rites,
I ignore divisions,
wave paradox
like a battle flag
in logic's face,
sidestep either/or,
choose both.

Convicted were Janice Hill, 24, and Margaret McGuire, 28, both of Philadelphia, Robert Smith, 32, of Media, former G E engineer William Whistler, 57, of King of Prussia; and the Rev. Vernon Schmid, 48, of Newark, Delaware

Spinning its fiery message,
the chariot dashes its magic
across the soul's eye:
"Stand up!"
You are sent
to stand as sentry
before the gates.
"Warn the people!"
And my mirror lights
with the demon's phallus
tipped with awful death,
sent by distant voices,
shuttle launched and free
burning shadows into stone,
evil's own memorial,
visible from your wonder
your own grey perch,
what is it in a son,
a priestly type,
to risk prison,
question authority
insist the American dream
failed long ago.
And you question:
"Where did we go wrong?"

Reihl Justice of the Montgomery County Court called the five members of the Media based Brandywine Peace Community, the ringleaders of the demonstration, wbich was organized to protest G. E 's development and manufacture of the Defense Satellite Communications System Phase III, a worldwide military communications system

"Where did we go right?"

[Newspaper quotes from The Philadelphia Inquirer, 1985]

Train Ride To Albany

Hills on the Hudson's far
west bank squat like fat
green women pounding
laundry clean against dark
river rocks, while vacationing
New Orleans women chat
about Manhattan taxi rides,
bars visited, all-night delicatessens,
shopping at Saks, without
reference to husband or home.

They are coeds again prowling
for laughs and, perhaps,
a one night stand, young hard
flesh pressed against them
in summer nights without names.

"Last night," they say,
"We walked the city at 2 a.m."
The conductor says, "You are
lucky to be alive." One, her
dark eyes suggesting she has no fear,
settles in her seat, her tan skin,
bobbed black hair highlighted
by white blouse and shorts.

I cast glances toward her,
picturing sex on a train.
She stirs, looks at me, smiles.
Caught, I look westward
toward the fat, green, squatting
women pounding the morning clean.

The Annunciation

When the messenger came
singing in Mary's womb
no one expected a messianic
revolution to follow.

The Nazareth house
of impregnation has disappeared.
Its memory, soiled by tall
steeples and insistent bells,

bejeweled stone and hanging
glitter, struggles to deny
the simplicity of Mary's
moment, vendors crying,

"Get your olive wood
statues of the Virgin here!"
"Special prices for visitors
who come to worship."

"Souvenir postcards,
ten for only a dollar."
Amen.

Talking With Daniel Berrigan About Poetry

[1985]

Speculating on what stands
examined by time,
worthy of effort, or not,
the old poet and I
discuss options..
No prizes come his way
these days. Radical
politics get in the way.
His prison stretches
taste bitter in the throat
of his critics. But
it is his choice. His
poet's heart refuses
to be choked by fear,
or jail, or academia.
So he carefully continues
threading words one after
another with a determined heart.
Tonight sitting before
my fire, he says, of poetry,
there are two kinds.
One is lived. The other
written by academics
for academics. It is
a statement for our time.
Of the two, the old
Jesuit says, his prairie
eyes glinting, he
favors the first.

Seducing A Poet In Tulsa

After a poetry reading in Tulsa
a voluptuous sixteen year old
sat across the table from me
asking questions about metaphors,
imagery and how does a poem mean.

Answering her in my most scholarly
manner, I noted a charming twinkle
in her eye and her foot in my lap
moving slowly and gently as it
massaged my disturbed crotch.

Inquisitive to a fault she remained
long after others left, her lips
moistened by a pink tongue as she
smiled and bid me come to her bed.
Encouraged by her love of poetry
and her foot I returned her smile.

Now, somewhere in Oklahoma
two freshly bathed feet await
the gentle touch of a nail polish
brush and says one foot
to the other, "I once seduced
a poet. What have you ever done?"

Cock-A-Doodle-Doo

I am told the Vikings know
about death without witness.

They say when a human
dies a white cock crows,

then a red cock crows,
then a black cock crows.

I wake each morning my ear
cocked for a trinity of sound.

Big Hats

"Geography blended with time equals destiny."
Joseph Brodsky

Old men in big hats squint and talk,
wide brims pulled low to shade
their eyes from the sun bleeding
down against the far horizon.

They talk with one jaundiced eye
cast toward a lean and hungry
boy frozen like a toad in stone,
beside dusty, rutted summer roads,

were tall, sweating and cursing men
pitch hay sky-wide and wagon-high.
No one suspects him, shirtsleeve ragged,
frayed denim and elbow patched.

The hayers do not know his purpose.
If they think at all in their task,
they think him touched, hunkered
with blazing eyes seeking constancy,

yet, frail as a spider's spinning,
while horses drag buckrakes to feed
the baler's hungry, gaping yaw.
The big hats do not know the mystery

calling him out in dog day heat to squat,
a summer haunt, restless as August dust
beside bitter streams running dark
as secret places of the once found heart.

Raucous frogs taunt from hiding,
like the James gang in Ozark caves,
or hermit monks singing rough matins
until time awakens to the light,

a shining ax splitting late shadows,
as the dark boy squats by a smoldering

smokeless fire, shaping conspiracies,
pledging hearts for the coming sacrifice.

2.

The big hats cough and nod, shift
chews of Red Man in their jaws,
offer the August dust a well placed
spit-brown volcano, one eye

fixed on the angry sky, the other set
to shatter the sun. Big hats know much.
They have watched the stars come.
They have watched the stars go.

They know the long angry prairie sea.
like Coronado, their restless souls
sought Quivera, faces too late shaded,
now lost in tall prairie grass memories,
these courthouse benchsitters,
ragged backyard fence-hangers,
coffee shop idlers, doughnut dunkers,
dead dick's along death's row,

call back the past, as if it were
here and now, making it stand
memory tall, while they pull Barlow
knives from patched overall pockets,

whittle shavings thin enough
to see through. The big hats
talk about the Kansas weather;
how it was hotter in the old days;

how winters froze them in fields
crisp as shards of November ice
in morning troughs. And they repeat
old saws and familiar sayings.

"The only thing between Kansas

and the North Pole is a barbed wire fence."

"I ain't afraid of hell.
I spent a summer in Kansas."

"Think it'll rain?"
"Be a hell of long dry spell if it don't!"

They brave again all the dangers.
Aging big hats tilted against the wind
recalling images of pain and joy,
celebrating each infrequent victory.

And when the old wooden bridge,
crossing Labette Creek west of town,
rumbles, they shake withering heads
and wonder about the young leaving,

bound for Wichita or Tulsa, Kansas City
or some other such exotic place
more distant than their dreams.
the big hats pause and speculate.

Some say the young left their souls
sitting empty as a drunkard's gut.
Some say the farms turned sick, vomited,
staggered, and died without benefit of God

or clergy. Some say the Great Depression,
dust bowl deep and bread line long,
still hangs heavy around weary necks,
fracturing souls like hammer to stone. .

Some say it was just God's will.
Others know better and say so.
Still others say nothing, silent faces
dark as the sky, tasting morning rain.

3.

Trotlines taut across the river,
the big hats and the boy gather

beside a midnight fire. The big hats
drinking long and deep from jars

filled with raisin-jack, while they
weave stories familiar as their brew.
The boy holds his breath and listens
to awful tales dancing in shadows

cast high against the cottonwoods
beside the sluggish, dark Neosho River.
catfish, larger than a man's arm,
they say, lurk in the murky waters.

Beyond the reach of human hands,
they are too smart to be hooked.
One man, they say, drowned while noodling;
reaching his hand deep into a hole

beneath the water of the river bank.
Their voices hush as they tell of it
so not to disturb the ghosts of those
still resting deep in the fishing hole.

A fish grabbed his hand, they say,
took him deeper than a man can go.
The boy listens and wonders about it,
the mystery of the deep, dark water

teasing his scarred imagination,
turning his mind to possibilities
darker than the night that holds them,
invisible as God's graceful hands.

Last Rites for a Teen Suicide

Clumsy as grief,
words cannot conjure up
balm for the healing.
Grace, perhaps,
will do the trick.
Or, so we pray,
our words slamming
against death
harder than anger.
Mercy may have to suffice,
ragged child that it is,
Weighing life
like a silent jury,
a jester priest
comforts with his cross,
shadowy hand sagging
across his greying heart,
as if it matters.

Dead Man's Cross

Cross arm bound to staff
by a cracked and dried thong,
it marks the spot where
a man fell and died.

Coming home from a long
day fishing, he staggered,
dropped the oar he carried,
tumbled into a heap.

His one lonely act, the one
we must someday share,
now is illuminated by a single
candle's evening glow.

Ancient Mexican shadows
touch the cross and road
as other fishermen pass by,
tipping battered straw hats.

Vernon Schmid

Sonnets For My Father

1

It is always you, your haggard
Mouth where laughter seldom
Stopped to grin. Your towering
Presence forcing me to look up.
It is always you, standing hard
Between me and childhood liberties,
Essential as they are for sanity.
I still tremble when I hear you,
Your voice iced with unreasonable
Anger shouting for my consideration.
I like to think I have your number.
I want to believe I have beaten you.
But late at night, with Wagner
Ringing in my ears, I beg for mercy.

2

Some say Kansas winters are cruel.
But, there was something in you
That was crueler than the tons of ice
Ripping limbs from elm trees to block
Our farmstead lane when I was twelve.
One sultry evening, after I came
Home from the army, and a coonhound
Failed to come when you called,
Your cruelty reached unexpected levels
As you beat her until I stepped in.
Then, you tried to beat me. Slamming
Your massive fist against my jaw.
Later, you came to me to ask pardon.
But, the wound was at home in my heart.

3

Perhaps, my love of good sausage
Is genetic, since you, too, loved good
Sausage. Perhaps, it is an indication
Of our ancestral code. Kneeling
Before trees they prayed for light,
Hard eyed as they faced the winter,
Sausage lovers all. We now kneel
Before our own gods while we wait
For the light of winter solstice to melt
The ice between us and bring us down
The Rhine of our own springtime,
Listening to children laugh at twilight
As we struggle in our clumsy way

4

Some things you simply do not let go.
Today I saw you again in the distance,
Your early grey hair lighting up the sky.
Your mother's hair, they tell me.
The same hair with which I am thatched.
You were standing behind Barney and Goldie,
Brown and chestnut monster horses
Dragging tons of cinder blocks on a sled,
Sweat lathering the places where harness
Rubbed their hairy hide. At first I refused
Belief. I know my wounds are deep.
Then I heard the shouts, the crowd
Hurrahing the team as you crossed the line.
And I exited the dream through my scars.

5

I never saw you naked except
That one afternoon after mother
Rose for morning ablutions and fell

Forward into the pitch black of death.
At the graveside you let me take you
Into my arms as you wept, shoulders
Shaking vulnerable for the first time,
A man who believed the wounded
Keep going, dragging their long guts
After them. I think it was then that
You reached your own katabasis.
Crop failures, poverty, a tattered soul
Patched as your bibbed overalls,
Had been overcome. This could not.

6

You were a two-sided father:
Coarse and hard, gentle
And generous. One side
Always visible. The other
A private matter. It is said
You never read a book. If
True, there was not a need.
You were a book. Your pages
Filled with warrior legends,
Your life a poem of pain, a
Sonnet of love, a hard-scrabble
Dance in Uncle Theodore's loft
With the croak of the fiddle
And Henry Morris' banjo twang.

7

Like dime store gawdies
Sparkle dims and time,
Caught in silver baskets,
Silhouetted you walked
Stooped toward the sun.
Mother watched from her rocker,
Knowing you when you stood tall,

Before eighty-nine winters
Claimed you, called you to account.
She smiled as you walked
Toward the sun bleeding out.
She remembered how you once
Held her in rough arms, took her
Heart and cradled it in love.

8

Like our hands we stood,
Leather and steel, father and son,
Tall and determined, fragile,
Tattered, flanking the wagon,
Splitting husks, snapping
Corn loose, banging each ear
Against the wagon box. The horses
Moved slowly, pulled the wagon
One step at a time not to get ahead
Of we huskers. It was a job
To be done each autumn when
Stalks, browning and brittle,
Matched the sap seeking
Sleep before winter snow.

9

Your grey hair meant what it said.
Every long furrow you plowed,
Every trip into those lead and zinc
Mines, every mile on the long
Roads were registered in your
Heart's logbook. Now you sit
On another porch watching the sun
Set and counting the wishing stars.
Some said your grey hair was a sign.
You were too old for the race, too
Tired for the hay-field hoorahs,

Too distant from boyhood victories.
Kansas winters aside, your grey hair
Sparkled with the challenge.

10

Mythology tells us female stones
Remain attached to the mountain.
Male stones are those that move
Beyond the mountain to singularly
Stand like Easter Island megaliths,
Stonehenge, or Irish dolmens,
Free from the mountain that gave
Them birth. You were such a stone.
You once stood tall and bone-raw
Over the dwelling place of time.
Now, when I visit your grave
I lie upon it and howl as I seek
My own place to stand, grey-bearded,
Freed from my distant mountain.

11

You always walked on the edge
Balance always in question,
Denouncing that beyond your grasp.
Now you use a steel walker,
A cage to hold you upright,
A cage for your spent rage.
You are not quite the same.
Any fool could note it. And,
If truth has its way, you
May not hear this poem posted
To you. Deadly news arrives
Regularly, whispers and grins
At my careening, frustrated heart,
Scarred by my own kept rage.

12

When I see a freshly turned field,
I smell you as I did when I was a boy.
Sweat, yours and the horses, fill
My nostrils. And I feel your hands,
Huge and rough, hanging from arms
I thought would never end. Tonight
I felt the rough denim of your overalls,
Heard the size twelve high topped shoes
Clomp across the kitchen linoleum
Toward the sagging huge corner chair
Where you sat to remove them, dirt
Smudges on your worn, white socks
Warning us of the odor soon to follow
As you sighed and closed your eyes.

Otium Sanctum

The place is secret,
founded in purity,
cast as God's love.
It is spirit delicate
as time spilling, sun
drenched, over walls
to flee. Holy leisure
is not for the asking,
but for the loving;
It demands unity.
It listens for God.

Cantina

Indigo all the sky, all the house of gold.
How it poured into me, the sun, through my eyes!
-Alfonso Reyes

Young men with old
eyes lean against the wall,
waiting for a miracle
that never happens,
waiting for a golden
angel who stands at the bar,
orders drinks all around and then
is gone. The sad men
know the angel is a dream.
They wait, nevertheless,
their patience heavy
as the mid-day sun from which
they hide, their faces drawn
long as Baja shadows.
Fearless cockroaches
amble across the floor;
big, handsome cockroaches
with human faces who watch
the young men flee from time
to time. But the young men
do not stay away for long,
for they do not know
when the angel may again
appear out of the desert,
or perhaps, from the Cortez
sea east of town where the water
opens an azure heart to the sky.
For now, they wait, praying
That when the angel comes,
they will find him good.

Witches At The Brew

"Whenever two people kiss the world is bom."
- Octavio Paz

Lying flank to thigh
against my wrinkled
substance, young breasts
pushing against
my heavy chest,
pouting lips wet from kisses
in the secret night,
dark-skinned lovers
sleep again in my bed,
stir my dreams
like witches at the brew.
I blame old age
or its shuddering memory,
my long ago ears
ringing with mariachi music,
my long ago tongue tasting
dark red wine sucked
deep and burning
with passion's dance,
splendid as an Indian serape.
My long ago heart,
fluttering old captive,
deep and dark as the soul,
leaps to touch memories
warm and wet as Baja's tidal
beaches curving tight against
the turquoise sea,
teaspoon lovers in time.
I am Hernan Cortez.
I have chosen Mexico.
I have burned my ships.
I have held life's blood
against the throb of thighs.
It is not gold that drew me.
It was tenderness.
Now, their faces refuse me.
In dream and waking
those who have been known
are no longer knowable.

Those who sucked
life from destiny's
deep well do not surrender
name or glint of eye.
They remain in shadows,
offering only a touch,
their breath hot as nights
in July back seats
of battered old Fords,
or in hideouts,
one eye poised,
a lookout for husbands
or angry lovers.
Like revolutionaries
waiting for the federales,
they come unafraid
waking me with kisses,
teasing my fragile heart,
calling me home to sit
elbows on table scooping
beans and rice with tortilla fingers,
listening as they make promises,
tell me not to cry,
hold me close,
sing quiet little songs,
lullabies late at night
as we lie exhausted,
a meld of bodies,
Heman and Marina
beneath the peeling paint
of yesterday's ceiling.

Capernaum

A bone for sunburned tourists to gnaw,
pilgrims stand open-mouthed,
Kodaks in hand, guide books opened,
reading about Jesus, Peter and the others.
Are they seeking understanding and wisdom?
In the Book it is reserved for the aging and women.
Clustered now they stand and whisper,
revering the synagogue's sandy ruins,
stone upon crumbling stone kneeling,
heads bowed before time, ravaged
by sun and wind, the Galilee held at bay,
its blue catching milky, wondering eyes
that stare from beyond cracked marble
columns at a single boat passing under sail.

The Armadillo

Defying the raging sun the nine-banded armadillo
Slips quickly through the shadows of Cirio trees,

A lumbering tank plowing past yucca plants crowned
With brilliant summer fire. Neither greasewood,

Nor elephant trees, deter his hungry mission.
When trapped, he becomes an armored ball,

His soft underbelly safe from cut of knives,
Or angry, stubborn claws. One with the armadillo,

I, too, plod past wind worn granite laced with rattlesnakes,
Lizards beneath my twisted feet, grey gringo beard

Shaded by a wide-brimmed palm-leaf hat snatched
From a busy mercado in Zapata's mountains. Unlike

The armadillo in appetite, however, I do not search
For carrion or ants. I have no taste for worms.

My hunger is deeper. It is passionate and desperate.
Vulnerable as the armadillo, grey tufts peeking

Through my scaled armor marking the places
Where knives may find their way deep into my heart,

Spreading blood and guts before waiting beaks of black
Robed vultures, or critics seeking an easy meal.

Taking my lead from brother armadillo, I seek refuge,
Burrowing deep into the sands of language.

Manhattan Breakfast

Cafeteria eggs before me,
I juggle ***The Times,*** swallowing
quickly, until I see his haggard face
expressionless through glass
dark enough for St. Paul, clear
enough for my own judgment.

Coat patched with tape,
quilt of poverty gathered
from garment district bins,
he rubs a bristling cheek,
notes my discomfort, smiles,
and fades into the crowd

Holocaust

After thirty years she stares
From dark photographs
Collected in a theater of terror,
Her supple body covered
With tatters, her erotic eyes blank
Behind cruel barbed wire.
Smelling dry leaves, I
Hear the sound of crickets,
Where we sought pleasure
Beside an autumn Kansas lake.
Today I recoil at the sight of her.,
Wishing I could reach her again.
It is confession I desire. I cannot
Deny complicity. I devoured her,
fractured our souls with pleasure.
Now, throat burning, my mind dances
To awful melodies as autumn blends
it smells with the smoke of stacks.

Poem

Watch them dance.
Words stepping
one behind another,
swirling skirts,
tapping heels,
sinners searching
for a ballet.

Eros

Un-American as I am,
it is an inward garden
I desire, filled with smoke,
dangerous fire,
ashes cooled only by
a long dark Kansas night
mixed with sweat,
sweet breath and danger.
I know it is not proper.
Many say we must not dwell
on things nestled deep within us.
It weakens resolve.
It might make us a nation of whiners.
Un-American as I am
I point out to them,
one finger extended,
that I desire to spend my life
amid flames, a burning heart,
scaring away the foolishness
they would have us choose.

Dead Man's Cross

Cross arm bound to staff
By a cracked and dried thong,
It marks the spot where
A man fell and died.

Coming home from a long
Day fishing, he staggered,
Dropped the oar he carried,
Tumbled into a heap.

His one lonely act, the one
We must someday share,
Now is illuminated by a single
Candle's evening glow.

Ancient Mexican shadows
Touch the cross and road
As other fishermen pass by,
Tipping battered straw hats.

Left Brain / Right Brain

Having grown tied of my
old left brain sitting on its
confused chair quoting
classical analysis, haunted
by reality cold as a shroud,
I chose to live with my
right brain, took the old
left brain out, left it sitting
in a field in Missouri
patching together formulas
and policies atop a missile
silo, child of its own making.

Monet's Zuiderkirk

(Philadelphia Museum of Art, 1987)

Even though I whispered my query
the painting of the Zuiderkirk
would not reveal if the Zuider
flowed in, out, or around the kirk.
God's grace came to mind,
demanding the same illumination.

For Ernesto / for Nicaragua

(On receiving a letter from Ernesto Cardinal, 1985)

The poet no longer writes.
Solitename sits silent in the sun.

Time does not permit the pen
so he notes in his letter to friends.

Cries heard in the night differ
from death's cries heard before.

In these nights the cries know pain
twisted in the gut by *El Norte.*

The poems are not the same as before.
Then they rested in passionate arms.

Now they insist on patience and prayer.
The poet no longer writes.

Looking For The Enemy

Red faced, beer gut bloated,
the sergeant stood fingers fixed,
an instrument of death.

It is simple, he said.
Two stiffened fingers
hard into the solar plexus
and driven up bursts the heart.

Or stick them hard into Adam's apple.
Either way, you win. The enemy dies.

Quick to learn I keep the skill,
coiled like a jaguar set to spring
on unexpecting prey.

In rooms filled with poets, or madmen,
priests or lunatics, I keep a watchful eye
looking for the enemy we were promised.

Last Testament

"Extinguish these miseries,
Since no else can stamp them out;
And may my eyes behold you,
Because you are their light,
And I would open them to you alone."

-John of the Cross

Being less than sound
in mind and body,
age slipping a rough
hand into my weeping bowel,
I wrestle to remain here.
Take me home for final sleep.
Let me rest in my own
middle kingdom close
to the center of the earth
that bore me to life.
Put me down beside
my mother and father.
Let dark and bloody
Kansas claim its own.
And as the light
fades on that epochal
hill keep no one away.
Invite brother pain to come
stand by my unsettled grave.
We are joined hip to hip
like Jacob and his comrade
wrestling in the mud.
And, if an accounting is in order,
as well it may be,
read the prosecution's case,
taking time to recall one
who lived placing words
one behind the other,
knowing that Coatlicue,
with her necklace of human hearts,
hands and stoney skulls,
possessed death's holy secret.
With due consideration

I prefer her mysterious dance.
1, too, reject the judgment
taught by long-faced
priests, who now rot
beneath bougainvillea idols.
They feared death's kiss.
Demanded bent knees
before the blood red cross,
denied truth and kissed
the twisted feet of their singular,
anguished and twisted Christ.
Like the Aztecs I choose to believe
death contains no fear of hell.
It is only death. God's final grace.
I do not want faulty prayers.
I invite you to come, dance
on my new-turned grave.
And just before katydids sing
a final hymn let the mariachis come
playing trumpet and guitar,
feet planted firrmly on the rich,
loose soil of my making.
Stained by flickering candles,
let the mourning rest. Share the picnic.
Spill the blood red wine.
There must be wine. And sing
while you dance on the day of death.
And let it be said loud
enough for the kingdom people
who cup their hands to hear:
"The poet did not betray."
That is enough.